Bil Keane

FAWCETT GOLD MEDAL • NEW YORK

A Fawcett Gold Medal Book
Published by Ballantine Books
Copyright © 1982, 1983 by Cowles Syndicate
Copyright © 1987 by King Features Syndicate, Inc.

Library of Congress Catalog Card Number: 87-91539

ISBN 0-449-12427-4

Manufactured in the United States of America

First Edition: December 1987

"Mmmm! That's music to my nose!"

"Mommy sure has a lot of hang-ups—'Hang up
your shirt, hang up your sweater . . .' "

"I know why we say grace. It's to let our food cool off."

"Thinking is when the picture is in your head
with the sound turned off."

"Grandma hates to clean bowls so I hafta help her out!"

"They shouldn't have been dropping that bread. That's littering!"

"We wouldn't need these if E.T. lived here."

"Which one are you saying 'no' to, Mommy?"

"Daddy said no on the 10-speed bike, so I'm going over his head."

"Why do store ladies always hafta push so many BUTTONS?"

"Let's tell each other what we want for Christmas."

"We rode on a REAL bus! Not just a school bus."

"There's one left over. Can you mail it to me?"

"Tell Aunt Nancy I've got all the clothes I need."

"We've watched enough Christmas specials for
tonight, Mommy. Guess we'll brush
our teeth and go to bed."

"Let's get one that's real wide at the bottom so there'll be room for lots of presents."

"What did you tell Santa?"
"I told him you'd put a check in the mail."

"Look, Mommy! I cleaned my plate!"

"... Three French heads, two turtle
dogs, and a ...."

"I don't hafta go back to school till
NEXT YEAR!"

"You creatures aren't s'posed to be stirring."

"We're not hungry, Mommy. Do we HAFTA
eat breakfast?"

"We forgot to put baby Jesus in the manger on Christmas Eve, Mommy. He's still in the drawer."

"It's what I've been wanting my
WHOLE LIFE!"

"Has anyone seen the floor?"

"No, that isn't a word either."

"He's in the bathroom mumbling at
the scales."

"Have I been good so far this year?"

"Where does it say 'To be continued
tomorrow night'? "

"I feel like I'm inside a shark!"

"It's pasghetti. You have to boil it
to get it to relax."

"Know what I'm going to name my new
doll? Polly Esther."

"I didn't even ask my question!"

"He's mad 'cause his 'Slinky' won't
go upstairs!"

"If God wanted me to play the piano he'd
have given me 88 fingers."

"But, we're gonna put the whole roll back when we're done."

"PJ closed the door when we told him to.
He's finally getting tamed."

"I like this kind of guitar music—one
thread at a time."

"We're makin' braces for our teeth."

"Let's see—it's 20 past one...from 6:45
to 12 is 5¼ hours, plus...say
1½ hours, that's...."

"Give me a high five, Daddy."

"Mommy! Can you come put the cartoons back on?"

"Stop talking, Dolly. I want to listen
to it snowing."

"I wish Kittycat was like Garfield so we could know what she's thinking."

"Can I have some dry gloves, Mommy?
These are full of snow juice."

"What does that sign say, Daddy?
Daddy?"

"Daddy, have you got any wood I
can use these nails on?"

"Can I wear my soap to school?"

"We're learnin' the albaphet. It's
just like the ABC's."

"How come you've never made friends
with anybody whose name
begins with a 'Z'?"

"Barfy's cold and wants us
to come in."

"Mommy's name was Carne before she
got married. What was
yours, Daddy?"

"Does this count for PJ's nap, Mommy?"

"You could read us the comics if you want
to, Granddad. But we're not allowed
to ask you."

"I don't think Grandma's havin' much
fun here. Let's play some games
with her."

"Granddad's mowing his face."

"Don't worry, Grandma. Mommy says
he's growin' like a weed, so
it'll fit him next week."

"But, if you came home with me, Love,
who would help Mommy take care
of Jeffy and PJ and . . ."

"Did God invent HEARTS for Valentine's Day
or was it Cupid?"

"Willard Scott's forecasts aren't always
100 percent accurate."

"Smear some jelly on your face. It keeps
her from kissin' you."

"Will somebody turn down this banana
for me, please?"

"The Japanese have the right idea."

"How do you KNOW each snowflake is different?
They all look alike to me."

"If Mommy and Daddy ever split, I'm
stayin' with her."

"Who gave me this shirt, Mommy?"

"Mommy, can we have some candy?"

"What do you push to make them sing?"

"I taught PJ how to go potty by himself. He just needs you to get him out."

"Why are we cooking trees?"

"Ah! My bed! My good ol' friendly bed."

"When you and Daddy ordered me was I in
stock or did you have to put me
on back order?"

"I didn't eat my banana 'cause it's burned."

"Daddy, what were you before you were a daddy?"

"Why wouldn't you read me what it said on the wall, Daddy?"

"Look! That newspaper thinks it's a kite!"

"Mommy, can I have some more peas?"

"Mommy! They're starting to redecorate
the birdhouse!"

"I got peanut butter on John Denver."

"How much did you win, Mommy?"

"How am I s'posed to love my neighbor when
she didn't even order any of
my candy bars?"

"Who pushed him?"

"Why is that silly man blowing his horn?"

"Billy said the 'm' word! He said 'meanie!'"

"Disco some more, Daddy!"

"My breath keeps gettin' in the wrong holes."

"They must be Easter eggs. They're blue!"

"Listen to what I learned:
Do-Re-Mi-Fatso-La-Ti-Do!"

"Daddy! Your compass is on 'empty!'"

"Mommy's countin' to 10!"

"They're not 'mushed' potatoes, Jeffy.
It's 'SMASHED' potatoes."

"Mommy, who invented jellybeans — the Easter Bunny or President Reagan?"

"They wear stripes to make themselves look taller."

"Daddy! The Easter Bunny's here already!
APRIL FOOL!"

"Can I eat this, Mommy? I don't see any germs on it."

"How much longer till we goeth home?"

"None of Jeffy's stuff is chocolate. How
did the Easter Bunny know Jeffy's
'lergic to chocolate?"

"My knees can't see out anymore."

"You talked to it too much."

"Which movie was this one in?"

"I can tell time now. It's one, two, three, three o'clock."

"You'd get muddy, too, if you were this
close to the ground."

"Ambulance! I stepped on an ambulance!"

"PJ's playin' in some leftover rain."

"Mommy, will you put some hairspray on my
shoelaces so they won't keep
comin' untied?"

"Go real slow, Mrs. Crisp. I haven't finished my homework."

"How do you know E.T. likes liver?"

"Mommy, will you hold the ramp for me?"

"It's time you learned: 'NO' is a complete sentence."

"Can I wear my short-sleeve pants?"

"I like reading. It turns on pictures in your head."

"Grandma likes that kind of music where
four barbers sing together."

"Look at Kittycat snoozin' in the sun.
She's bein' solar heated."

"These little hunks of toast are hard to sink."

"I hope I don't have to send anybody else to his room."

"Come on, Daddy. You said we were going to
roto-tilt the garden today."

"I think it has a child-proof top."

"That smell gives me an idea, Mommy. How about making some lemonade?"

"Hi, Mrs. Lincicome. Could my Mommy borrow some bread crumbs, an onion and a cookie?"

"We should only talk to strangers if we
know them. Right, Mommy?"

"Are you finished yet? Can I touch it now?"

"I must've left the window open and a tornado got in."

"How many days till tomorrow?"

You can have lots more fun
with
BIL KEANE and
THE FAMILY CIRCUS